T0130494

# The I Hate Trump Book

## Then, Now and Forever

## Richard Castellane

Copyright © 2021 by Richard Castellane. 823361

All rights reserved. No part of this book may be reproduced
or transmitted in any form or by any means, electronic or
mechanical, including photocopying, recording, or by any
information storage and retrieval system, without permission
in writing from the copyright owner.

The views expressed in this work are solely those of the author
and do not necessarily reflect the views of the publisher, and
the publisher hereby disclaims any responsibility for them.

To order additional copies of this book, contact:
Xlibris
844-714-8691
www.Xlibris.com
Orders@Xlibris.com

ISBN:	Softcover	978-1-6641-4654-9
	Hardcover	978-1-6641-4655-6
	EBook	978-1-6641-4653-2

Library of Congress Control Number:	2020924291

Print information available on the last page

Rev. date: 12/07/2020

Dear Reader,

After multiple letters to the editor, many of which have been published, I've hit the end of my rope. My hatred of Don the Con Trump knows no bounds. I have spent time in countries with repressive governments, but always the repression was clearly spelled out. Never in my wildest thoughts could I ever imagine that a two bit snake oil salesman could become president of the country I've held in such high esteem. I can recall being in a communist country-- some 50+ years back where there was American military response to Communist military action. Literally all of the young communists were patting me on the back because of what seemed at that time to be a lawful American military response to perceived North Korean aggression. They were cheering someone---me--who represented a position adverse to their political backgrounds. WHAT A CHANGE FROM THAT TIME TO THE PRESENT. UNDER THE IGNORANT COWARDLY ACTIONS OF OUR PRESIDENT WE HAVE LOST THE SUPPORT WE ONCE HAD AMONGST NATIONS. Trump has done it. There is only one answer to a Trump. Standing at the forefront of the answer to Trump is the fate of Benito Mussolini. He promised the Italian people that he would enrich them, make Italy great again. His actions demeaned the great traditions of the Italian people, and he paid the price. They were hung upside down from a metal girder above a service station on the square. The bodies were beaten, shot at, and hit with hammers. Food for thought, isn't it?

Richard Castellane
Munnsville, NY

**TO THOSE WHO OPPOSE THE TYRANT IN THE WHITE HOUSE**
I want allies.
Green, purple, white, black, brown.
I want allies to guard my flank from surprise attacks.
Allies who will support Democracy.
Allies I can break bread with, share a love of freedom with.
Share opposition to a dictator, that I may live.
More importantly, that Democracy may live.
The Presi-dunce in the White House is destroying my chances, your chances, for allies. And we haven't said a word about it until now.

**Query**: What are the words that come to mind when you hear the word "TRUMP"?

**Answers**: Disasters, depression, Hurricane Dorian (Suppressing Climate Change Science), Recession, migraine headaches, sleeplessness, stomach cramps, eczema, loss of libido, pimples, skin problems, heart attacks, flatulence, more flatulence, constipation, heart palpitations, diarrhea, hemorrhoids, cataracts, belly fat, double vision, triple vision, landslides, tornados.

**Suggestion**: Let's all get together and get rid of the present occupant of the White House. Highly necessary if we all want to get some sleep again.

**TO DON**

You're scr…ing us up Don, bad, real bad.

Maybe you should be gone, out of our faces.

Ya know, begone Don begone

How many acres in Red Square have you been promised, Don?

Should be prime real estate.

You're worth it – to them

In a recent tweet, Trump said: "***The concept of global warming was created by and for the Chinese in order to make U.S. manufacturing non-competitive.***" Really, Don? Are you now pushing Chinese restaurants - have a big stake $$$ in them?

**I Mourn for My Country.**

I mourn for the failure of our educational system to prepare opposition to a dictator, to prepare our young to see what a dictator is, does. How terribly sad that my countrymen and women do not understand the lessons of history. Can they even spell Hitler's first name, Set forth the country of his birth, the city of his attempted putsch, his favorite composer? If you ask, you get a blank dumb-dumb look. Such be our education of the young.

I'm not surprised that a tyrant in the White House can fool, obstruct, outsmart some 40% of our population. Oh, how I mourn for my country.

**Locked and Loaded**

Let's face it, our "locked and loaded" spouting President, who likes to flex phony muscle to support his wannabe macho man image, has dug us a deep hole. His on-going lies have made a joke of the term "Presidential credibility". Today, no one believes anything he says. Instead of hiding his face in shame, he struts about acting out an image of a belligerent rooster. Unfortunately, under the rooster's plumage, is a pot belly, ignorant, morally emaciated buffoon. Our enemies are having a field day with him – that's not good for us. They see our "locked and loaded" President for the fraud he is. This makes us much more vulnerable. I predict that the attack on the Saudi oil facility is just the beginning. The only answer – vote him out of office in 2020.

**I Can't Sleep**

If a group of Psychiatrists and Sleep Deprivation Doctors wrote this letter:

""Never had so much business. Seems our president enjoys stirring up anxiety, sleeplessness in the citizenry. Physical and mental damage to patients is enormous, but the perpetrator, President Trump, doesn't seem to care".

**Trump's Code, Calling for Civil War If He's Deposed**

By now, all have become familiar with Trump's statement on Sunday, September 29th :

"…If the Democrats are successful in removing the President from office (which they will never be), it will cause a civil war like fracture in this nation, from which our Country will never heal." Quoted from the original statement by Pastor Robert Jefferies (the Pro-Trump Megachurch Pastor from Texas, with a record of controversial and offensive comments, including calling Climate Change "imaginary", labeling Mormonism a cult, and saying "Jews will go to hell".)

The statement seemingly predictitory, without serious connotation, is ANYTHING BUT. It is a coded message by Trump to his followers (rightists, fascists, racists, nationalists) to resort to civil war if he, Trump, is removed from the Presidency. You read right, CIVIL WAR. Killing, guns, mayhem, end of our democracy…all embodied in Trump's call to his followers. This from the President of the United States. Unbelievable. The present occupant of the White House must be CONFRONTED, now more than ever.

**Self-Preservation in the Age of Trump October 2, 2019**

I am not alone. Millions stand with me in feeling that Donald Trump is a major threat to our existence, our survival. Trump's mental imbalance was, once again, clearly demonstrated in his 10/02/19 press conference. Major medical authority including (Dr. Bandy Lee, Yale Medical School, Dr. John Gartner, Yale Medical School, Dr. Bart Rossi, Fordham University, amongst others) have sounded the alarm that Trump's mental level is a clear and present danger to all of us. I believe I speak for the majority of American's when I say "life is precious to us, to our families, to our nation". That's a simple truth. If you believe what I've said, then how, I ask, can any of you support an unstable President who's shaking hand -- is over the nuclear trigger. The answer to this monstrosity in the making – remove Trump from the nuclear trigger, and restore pride in our nation, flag, values – and let us be able to go to sleep with a realization that we will wake up the next morning.

**Don the Con is a Nazi**

AMERICANS WAKE UP--BEFORE IT'S TOO LATE

He is a remnant Nazi, who has defied the passage of time-- who your grandfathers fought on the beaches of Normandy, at the Remagen Bridge, in the Hurtgen Forest, during the Battle of the Bulge. DON IS A NAZI, MAKE NO MISTAKE ABOUT IT.

**To The Mice Amongst Us**

You call yourselves Americans. A part of the land of the free, home of the brave. What a joke. You're about as brave as a gutless mouse, and as far as you being part of the land of the free, well, Don the Con (aka Trump) has daily rubbed your noses in his s---t and you let him do it--continually. Free? About as free as a German who criticized the Fuhrer in 1940.

What is most disturbing and indicative of gutlessness is your constantly addressing the con man as **Mr President**-- even after he ongoingly insults loyal Americans and our Constitution. The Con man deserves not an iota of respect. Designating him as "Mr. President" is to show homage, respect for one who constantly, unashamedly stands for the worst of all--PURE UNADULTERATED TYRANNY, ALSO KNOWN AS NAZIISM.

I feel **"DON THE CON"** is a much better designation. Your view?

**Heil Hitler, Heil Trump!**

**A Wake up Call to Republican Politicians**

"If there is any desire on your part to continue in governmental service--**heed the following:**

If, as seems very probable, your Donald is swept from office and by a landslide, your political status/clout goes bottom up. In other words you become **dead meat.**

If prior to the election you have taken positions supportive of "Don the Con's" fascistic, dictatorial, anti-US Constitution provisions, you will be noted as a "Trump-pet". You will reap the negative reward of having been supportive of a would-be dictator, a would-be king, a would-be NAZI. Such would be your political demise. But it need not be--if you now disassociate from "Don the Con"! **Not only will you be doing the right thing for Democracy, but at the same time you'll be preserving your future."**

**Voter Fraud**

Trump's interference with Americans' right to vote (ie. He's admitted motivation to interfere) is a criminal offense of a MOST SERIOUS NATURE. A massive number of states--through their Attorney General's offices must bring action against Trump. The statute dealing with the offense can call for, amongst other things, JAIL TIME (OF UP TO 12 MONTHS). Query, what is the Democratic leadership waiting for? Despite what Trump's hand picked judges might decide, there must be a public outcry, a scream of shattering proportions. There must be such if we are not to lose the last vestiges of a free society. Trump is a fascist dictator and we must get rid of him for the good of Democracy. The "UP TO 12 MONTHS IMPRISONMENT MUST BE FOLLOWED, SEEN TO ITS FULFILLMENT."


**An Awakening, a Reckoning**

Who is Donald Trump? Let me take a few moments to tell you,-- and hopefully you'll take a few moments to think it out.

The **Billionaire** who hides his tax returns from the American people so they don't learn the truth about his crookedness and connection/indebtedness to Vladimir Putin; the **Genius** who doesn't want the public to get a glimpse of his college grades because he paid a third party to take his SATs; the **Businessman** whose business knowhow led to three casino bankruptcies after chalking up losses of over one billion dollars, with investors losing their shirts at the same time ; the **Virus Expert**, who according to him, astounds scientists with his incredible scientific knowledge; the **Mental Genius** who suggests that if you want a cure for the Coronavirus you drink bleach(ie. Clorox) while at the same time shoving a light up your ass; the **Leader of the Free World** who states that he fell in love with Kim Jong-Un while at the same time promoting policies that will allow Iran to make nuclear bombs; the **Climate Control Denier** whose folly is the fundamental cause of California's shattering wildfires; the **Putin Lover** who colluded with Putin and Russian secret service operatives during the 2016 Presidential Election; the **Christian** who likes to wave the bible in front of cameras while at the same time violating every major principle of Christianity including the marriage vow where he had outside sexual relations while his wife was about to give birth; the **Patriot** who has committed treason by turning a blind eye on Russian bounties for killing American servicemen; the **Philanthropist** who creates charities and then steals from their proceeds; The **Warrior** who dodged the draft at least five times during Vietnam by projecting a phony excuse from a chiropractor doing a favor for the Patriot's father; the **Tough Guy** who uses makeup and hair coloring to give the illusion of youthful vitality; the **Denier** who under his watch has looked on while 180,000 Americans died, and 30,000,000 million became unemployed during the Corona onset; the **Genius** who mocked the wearing of face masks during the Corona epidemic, leading to the death of multi thousands who believed in the genius; the **Paragon of Fairness** who does his best to dismantle the United States Post Office so as to negate the voting of the opposition; the **Golfer** who upon documentation spends about one third of his governmental office time playing golf; the **Faker** who is refusing in advance to accept the election results if they don't go his way.

Even his claims that under him we have "the greatest economy ever" isn't even worthy of being called "full of shit". The economy in actuality is far down on the list of other presidents' accomplishments. Tellingly below the economic status achieved under President Obama.

The above is just a brief analysis of the Con Man's bullshit. The Con man who ongoingly claims that he's making America great again, and that whatever is wrong--he's the only one who can fix it, and this coming from a mentally ill individual suffering from PSYCHOPATHIC NARCISSISM.

**AND HE WANTS A SECOND TERM? THE ONLY SECOND TERM HE DESERVES IS A SECOND TERM IN A FEDERAL PRISON--WHICH IS MOST LIKELY TO OCCUR.**

**October 30, 2019**

Out of curiosity, I was interested in the background of Ambassador William Taylor an individual at the forefront of any potential impeachment, and removal from office, of Donald Trump. I knew nothing of Taylor until I did some research. Simply put, I was overwhelmed by Taylor's quality. Some of the more significant: Top 1% of West Point class. Harvard University School of Government, 101$^{st}$ Airborne Division during Vietnam (Bronze Star and Air Medal for Heroism), Commander 2$^{nd}$ Cavalry, Defense Advisor to U.S. Ambassador NATO, Ambassador to Eastern Europe and the former Soviet Union, Ambassador in Kabul, Director Iraq Reconstruction Office, U.S. Government representative Israeli Gaza disengagement, U.S. Ambassador Ukraine 2006 - 2009, Special Coordinator Middle East Transitions, Chargé d affaires for Ukraine in June 2019 when Trump attempted to extort the President there.

Taylor is the man who the MIDGET in the White House dares to confront.? A midget who has spouted some 14,435 documented lies. A midget who only excels in wrestling porno queens.

**Letter to the Editor**
**Utica Observer Dispatch**
**November 1, 2019**

Trump is a congenital liar, but even more serious, he suffers a mental illness called Delusional Disorder: delusions suffered by an individual in an unshakable belief in something that isn't true. These are delusions like being deceived, conspired against; or belief that someone is in love with them (i.e. – Trump on the North Korean dictator's letters – "we fell in love" over the "beautiful letters".) or grandiosity – over-inflated sense of worth, power, knowledge, talent. Trump's constant proclamation that he is a "stable genius" for example; or persecutory – that he's being spied upon by someone planning to do him harm. In May 2018, Trump broadcast that there was a spy in his 2016 Election Campaign and the spy received a "massive amount of money". No evidence to support this. Potential actions of such a sick individual? Slippage of a cruel, hateful individual's index finger over the nuclear button. Bing Bang Boom. A mushroom cloud for you, me, the world. BING BANG BOOM!

For survival's sake, vote him out of office.

Richard Castellane, Munnsville NY

Dear Richard,

Wow! Your editorial published in the Utica OD was powerful and thought provoking! Thank you for writing it. I have had the same thoughts as you should such a scenario occur. This man, who is occupying the White House, is an evil force in this country and the world. I agree with you 100% that he must not be re-elected in 2020. I hope that your words of wisdom will educate some of our citizens, enlighten them to the dangers that lay ahead, should he not be stopped.

With all my best wishes,<br>George Tulloch, Utica, NY

**On October 30, 2019 I submitted a letter to the editor.** The reason for the letter was my belief that the con man sitting in the White House would do everything he could to avoid leaving the White House--despite losing the election. I am more convinced now than ever that the scenario I wrote about over a year ago once again frighteningly looms over us as we approach the 2020 Presidential election. For all who wish the preservation of Democracy please go over the following letter. Hopefully your actions will be for Democracy--not for the dictatorship that Trump envisions for you.

**The Greatest Single Threat To Democracy Post-2020 Election. A hypothetical scenario:**

Trump loses the election. Whatever the margin of loss, small or great, Trump refuses to vacate the White House, claiming that he was cheated, that serious election irregularities fomented by leftist, socialist, communist, liberal elements of the democratic party -- have denied him what would have been an overwhelming victory.

Riots ensue. Trump supporters from the extreme right flood the streets, guns in hand. Trump presents himself in an emergency appearance on National TV, claiming that the Constitution is being threatened by liberal extremists. He claims, upon his obligation to the country, that his first duty is to protect the Constitution from the extremist attacks of socialists and communists. He calms the public by "assuring them" that he is supported by the U.S. Military, citing The U.S. Military Oath of Enlistment to his interpretation.

**Military Oath of Enlistment**
**"I, do solemnly swear that I will support and defend the Constitution of the United States** against all enemies, foreign and domestic; that I will bear true faith and allegiance to the same; and that I will obey the orders of the President of the United States and the orders of the officers appointed over me, according to regulations and the Uniform Code of Military Justice. So help me God."

(Title 10, US Code; Act of 5 May 1960 replacing the wording first adopted in 1789, with amendment effective 5 October 1962).

**Query**: It is obvious to this writer that if the President were to do something negative to the U.S. Constitution, the Military would be caught in a Catch 22. Are they, the Military, to support the President who has acted against the Constitution, or is the Military to oppose the President in defense of the Constitution?

The President will call upon the regular Army, National Guard, Reservists, to support his "defense of the Constitution". He will becloud the Catch 22 ambiguity in the oath to his interpretation.

**Result**: An ignorant military begins to clear the streets of anti-Trump elements while at the same time, Trump declares, on National TV, an emergency requiring imposition of Martial Law. From the womb of the above actions of the President, and our Military, a dictatorship is born. The great experiment in Democracy, begun some 243 years back, is now dead and buried.

Does the above scenario capture the mental mechanism, the dictatorial inclinations, of our President? I suggest you think long and hard on that question - **AND ACT ACCORDINGLY.**

## TAR & FEATHER HIM

That would be the very least that would happen a hundred years back to a lying politician. TAR AND FEATHER HIM BEFORE HE TOTALLY DESTROYS THIS COUNTRY! Actually I can think of different actions which would tend to discourage the gravedigger of Democracy "Don the Con Trump" Why is the Republican party so hesitant to deal with him. It would be deemed a Patriotic move, now and in the future. To end Trump's REGIME WOULD HISTORICALLY BE DEEMED THE HEIGHT OF PATRIOTISM.

## BIDEN MUST SET A TV EVENT

...Featuring a round table of ex-- Marine, Army, Navy generals and admirals who skewer Trump as a facist determined to tear down the Constitution. REPEAT REPEAT REPEAT!! The theme should be that Trump's mental illness (Malignant Narcissism) is heading us to a war that he'll be very sure to be protected from. Also project his avoidance of the draft by having his real estate father getting a tenant to write an excuse (for Trump to avoid the draft) that Trump has never fully explained. DRAFT DODGER, DEFILER OF THE CONSTITUTION, NEVER STOOD AGAINST AN ARMED ENEMY, A PHONY, A COWARD--WHO LIKES OTHERS TO PUT UP THEIR LIVES while his family bathes in luxury and out of harm's way.

## GOD BLESS AMERICA

From the day Trump became president of the United States, all matters affecting our daily lives have become worse, day by day. Our need for some form of reasonable normalcy has been resoundingly smashed by a president whose "tweets", hour by hour, sew disunity, violence and most significantly the weakening of all major aspects of our Democracy. We are becoming disunified, close to the point of no return. Daily tranquility, calmness, peacefulness, serenity are something we can only relate to as having occurred---in the past. It might be wise for the reader to ask him/herself how frequently during the presidency of Trump, have you had a good night's sleep—no mental anguish, no tossing or turning, no waking up in a cold sweat. Donald Trump is not only a national disaster, but upon his pathetic example as a leader, he has become an international one.

From my university days at Princeton I have always been interested in the rise of Adolf Hitler, his attaining the position of Reisefuhrer, his demise, and where he took the German people with him—DOWNWARD—IN DESTRUCTION. I SEE AN ENORMOUS SIMILARITY BETWEEN ADOLPH HITLER AND DONALD TRUMP. BEING FAMILIAR WITH HITLER'S POSITIONS AS TAKEN IN HIS "MEIN KAMPF" I say without hesitation that Trump is following Hitler's playbook very very closely. The lying, the cheating, the stealing, the demeaning, the falsities of Hitler are part of the Trump tactic. Our own naïveté in closing our eyes to what Donald Trump really is, will end up causing our own demise.

**GOD BLESS AMERICA---IF THERE STILL IS AN AMERICA AFTER THE ELECTION OF 2020.**

**President Trump has made more than 20,000 false or misleading claims**
*Here is his lie for today - ANOTHER LIE TO BE THROWN IN THE CESSPOOL OF TRUMP LIES!*

"I've rebuilt the military, 2.5 trillion dollars." And, "I got them raises like no President before!"

Trump frequently suggests this money is all for new equipment, but he's just adding together three years of budgets created by Nancy Pelosi and passed in the normal course of business.

**SUCKERS & LOSERS** September 5

When asked to honor America's fallen soldiers, Trump called those who have fought and died for our country "suckers" and "losers." He was more concerned about getting his hair wet than visiting a military cemetery. This draft-dodging president knows nothing of sacrifice, denigrates and disrespects the military, and is not fit to lead this nation.

**Trump's Chest Thumping**

How many of you, who viewed Trump's chest thumping at the killing of Al-Baghdadi, were deeply impressed by Trump's display of "manly delight" at the killing? His chest thumping was a symbol of manliness and righteous ferocity. Right? No, wrong!

Rather a display of Trump's on-going hypocrisy. In truth, Trump's chest thumping was by a full-blown coward, a draft dodger. How many of you have been impressed by Trump's awarding of Military medals to various individuals?

In fact, Trump avoided the military from the time he was first eligible to serve. His rich, connected, real estate developer father managed – UNDER VERY SUSPICIOUS CIRCUMSTANCES – to get a letter for medical deferment from one of Fred's tenants. It doesn't take much thinking to conclude that if you're the tenant for a very powerful landlord, you cooperate with what the landlord wants. In this case, it was a letter claiming that Fred's son, Donald, had a bone spur in his foot. That was all that was necessary for our "President" to get a medical deferment. The Podiatrist's daughters, during an interview, inferred that the diagnosis was phony. Surprising? Not really. Like daddy, like son. Weaving and bobbing around the truth.

### On Lieutenant Colonel Vindman
*A warning to you Trump.*

Trump! You shall immediately cease your evil attacks against American patriot, Lieutenant Colonel Vindman. You and your cronies attack him solely because he caught you in your quid-pro-quo lie, which, I believe, should sink you. Your lies, Trump, are like a rope winding more and more around your neck. Bravo, Lt. Colonel Vindman, you are a true American patriot.

**Shame on Us** November 1, 2019

Upon my return to Law School, a second career at 48 years of age, what overwhelmed me in my studies of Constitutional Law were the great decisions of our Supreme Court on due process, equal protection, and the 1st amendment. Humane decisions that filled me with wonder, at the humanity of our highest court, and of our country. I was proud to call myself an American. Since I was a traveler, worldwide, the occasions to proudly proclaim "I'm an American" were recurring.

40 years have caused a great change in my thinking. Our current President, with the assistance of politicians who have no idea of those wonderful decisions I've referred to, or the concepts of liberty within them, is piece by piece, upon his dictatorial tendencies, tearing apart the democracy I saw, respected, and admired. They made me proud to be an American.

Now, today. Enduring shame on Trump. Enduring shame on his supporters. And enduring shame on all of us, if we do not oppose, to the last of our strength, this dictator presently sitting in the White House.

**A New Low for Donald Trump** November 4, 2019

Once again, the present occupant of the White House has gone beyond law and beyond conscience. In on-going tweets, our White House con artist makes repeated calls for the "whistleblower" to identify him/herself. Trump knows full well that what he demands is against law, as per the Whistleblower Protection Act of 1989. Said law was passed by Congress to protect those brave individuals from the retribution of such as Trump, who use the Presidency for corrupt purpose. Trump doesn't give a hoot about the safety of that courageous individual who revealed Trump's illegal, immoral, illicit acts. If only his precious Ivanka was so exposed, our President would learn. Ivanka would also learn, to her mortal danger. Perhaps that's something that would wake up at least a piece of the conscience that might be in our President's soul.

HOORAH TO THE WHISTLEBLOWER, whoever he or she might be. The judgement of history will be overwhelmingly on the whistleblowers side. The judgement of history, on those members of the Republican congress who knowingly support the unconscionable actions of Trump, will be resoundingly negative. How dare Trump and his followers spit on our Constitution? From here on, I will proudly call myself "A WHISTLEBLOWER". Isn't it time for many of my readers to also call yourselves a WHISTLEBLOWER?

**Dictator At The Gate** December 19, 2019

The issues revolving around Trump are not complex. They're relatively simple. The FUNDAMENTAL issue is whether we want to trade living in a Democracy, to a life dominated by a Dictatorship. Germans faced such a question in the 1930's. They were fed a convincing line promulgated by one well known to all of us – Adolf Hitler. The Germans fell for his line. They suffered by yielding millions of lives to the grim reaper. By the end of World War 2, Germans knew - that the line they were being fed by the Dictator was not only false, but destructive. To understand what is going on today, you only have to substitute the form of Trump for that of Hitler. Simple, obvious, and a lesson that too many Americans appear to forget. I, for one, prefer living in a Democracy where government is beholden to the people, not the reverse. Trump is a danger beyond any we have faced. If his budding Dictatorship is not snuffed out, NOW, I predict that we'll face an even greater demolition of Democracy than did the German people face in following their Fuhrer. We must unmask Trump. Open your eyes.

**I Am Not a Trump-Pet** December 30, 2019

Ever since I saw Trump gleefully imitating a man suffering a severe mental/physical illness, I despised Trump. The cruelty that he exhibited in his imitation rendered him unfit for any position.

Today, news reported that Trump had tweeted the name/identity of the whistleblower who exposed Trump's impeachable offenses. The words of NPR's Bobby Allyn best describe my feelings:

"A callous and cruel disregard for the well-being of anyone one or anything untethered from his own personal needs and interests."

Trump's deed is once again evidence that he is the most unfit, unsavory individual to ever occupy not just the White House, but any position, government or non-government. Trump's action puts a target on the back of the named individual. A target, I suggest, far more suitable on the back of Trump.

How cruel, how evil this man. I hesitate to even call him a man, as his evil is unequaled in the history of our Presidency. I spit, with the fullest contempt, at his image. Let him go back where he came from. It's warm there, and I'm not talking about Mar-a-Lago.

al concept by Richard Castellane

**February 1**

*The following is extrapolated from a Thomas Jefferson letter to William S. Smith, dated November 13, 1787.*

"The people cannot be all, and always, well informed. If they remain quiet under misconceptions, it is lethargy, the forerunner of death to the public liberty.... And what country can preserve its liberties, if its rulers are not warned from time to time that …people preserve the spirit of resistance? The remedy is to set them right as to the facts. The tree of liberty must be refreshed from time to time, with the blood of patriots AND TYRANTS."

Ask yourselves the question, can Jefferson's directive be applicable to what we are confronting today?

**February 28**

With all that's going on with "Don the Con's" screwed up handling of a meaningful response to the Coronavirus piercing our borders- you can still be very sure of one thing. That the "Con Man's" made certain that Melania, Ivanka, Don Jr., Eric and Barron have already received the most updated protection to thwart the virus. Protections far beyond those "Don the Con" has authorized for the common people of the United States. That means you and me.

Now, Don's mealy-mouth serf, Mike Pence, receives appointment from the "Con Man", to be the Health Czar, to deal with the virus in the United States. Suggest it's time to fully pay up the costs of your burial plot. Now, more meaningful than later. Pence's training in the scientific world is next to nil. But Don doesn't care. Any bad news will be filtered through Pence, giving it the look- of purity. Just more of the same from the master of fake news- "DON THE CON".

The "Con Man" covers his butt when things go wrong by having a "yes-man" and crony (aka Pence) say the right things to protect the boss from accusations of incompetence and mismanagement in dealing with an epidemic that threatens every American, excepting of course, Melania, Ivanka, Don Jr., Eric, Barron and the "Con Man" himself.

What a joke. What an obvious cover-up.

They're all well protected from the virus by the "Con Man's" liberal use of tax-payer dollars to protect him and his own. Don't lose any sleep as to whether he is exposing him and his family to the very things he's exposing us to. Simply put, he doesn't give a damn about anything or anybody except him and his contemptuous brood.

Wake up Americans, if it's not already too late.

**A Good Night's Sleep** May 4

Upon Don the Con's ignorance, his refusal to even read the intelligence agency reports and his reliance on his diseased brain (superiority syndrome), trump is driving the American people into a full blown economic depression.

The money has run out. He is printing fake treasury notes and signing his name to fake IRS letters. The National Debt is out of control.

Wake up Americans! Restore reasonableness to our governance. We must get rid of the catastrophe sitting in the Oval Office so we can get a good night's sleep once again!

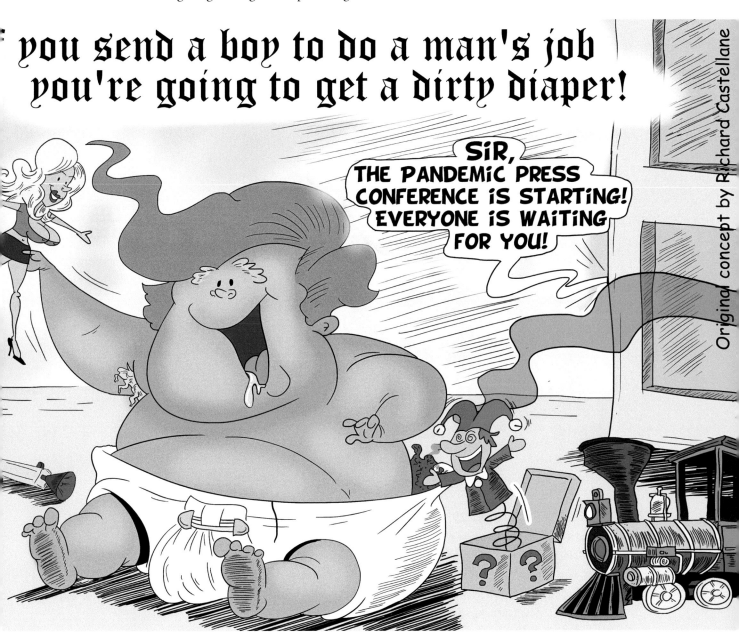

15

Original concept by Richard Cast[e]

**HE'S COUNTING ON IT** April 29

He's counting on it. And he just might be right.

He's counting on the memory span of Americans being so short, that by the time of the presidential election In November, Americans will have lost memory of how the con-artist, the self-anointed "Stable Genius" caused the deaths of thousands of Coronavirus victims. The cause being the "genius' " gross neglect to heed multiple warnings of the Virus' arrival. The warnings are well documented, including from his own daily briefings.

KEEP THIS IN MIND--- COME NOVEMBER!

**Grifter-in-Chief** March 5

The Trump Clan is stealing millions of our dollars from us. The Hunter Biden matter is a piss in the bucket compared to what the Trump Clan is doing to us. Right before our eyes we are seeing grand theft, on a scale previously unimaginable. The Trumps and their entourage are living the grand life while the average American must struggle just to make ends meet. By way of example, Jared Kushner can't get a security clearance, yet upon Don-the-Con's "influence" he is free to make personal deals with the Qatar Government for investment in his real estate empire - in illegal exchanges for US weapons' sales. The Saudis get boots (American Soldiers) on the ground in exchange for their personal investment in Trump world. Are those soldiers (your sons and daughters) put in harm's way? You can bet on it.

Yet more. Jared and Ivanka made $165 million last year and $220 million the year before, 2,550 times more than the average American family's yearly income. Amazed? Shouldn't be. You're being ripped off by the master con-artist and his brood.

Ivanka Trump, won initial approval from the Chinese government for 16 new trademarks, covering a wide range of products that include voting machines. This occurred while her father continues to wage a trade war with China. The trademarks for Ivanka Trump-branded products include nursing homes, sausage casing, handbags, shoes, wedding dresses and jewelry. Those trademarks are worth millions—all to go into the pockets of Trump and his brood.

Trumps' sons Donald Jr and Eric have cost us, you and me, $250,000 PER MONTH for their travel and security. With amazing chutzpah, they charge the US Secret Service $650 PER NIGHT to stay in one of their own hotels. Amazed? Infuriated? YOU SHOULD BE. When the con-man's sons travel overseas ON FAMILY BUSINESS? US taxpayers, you and me, foot the bill for hundreds of thousands of dollars in hotels, airfare and other costs for Secret Service protection, including $15,000 a night SPENT AT A TRUMP-BRANDED PROPERTY IN IRELAND. Me thinks even the little green-coated leprechauns thereabouts got stomach-upset from the Trump Clan's ripoff—of us.

It's way past the time to restore American honor and integrity. All of the groups mentioned in this letter must present themselves for congressional investigation. We must demand a public hearing in the House of Representatives - allowing all the facts to come out.

I own a Jack Russell Terrier. The breed is noted for going into a hole and pulling out a fox. My Jack Russell will just as readily pull out a rat. I donate his services to fulfilling that quest.

The answer, in a few short words, SUBPOENA THEM, SUBPOENA THEM, SUBPOENA THEM, SUBPOENA THEM. They seek to bring Hunter Biden before them for next to NOTHING. Let's subpoena the true culprits to bring them before Congress—for what is really SOMETHING.

# Bolton Reveals Trump's Deal Making Prowess in New Bo

Original concept by Richard Castellane

**Stable Genius?** March 18

Trump fired America's pandemic response team! Demand he reassemble it to confront the coronavirus pandemic immediately!

The consequences of the President and his team's monstrously selfish attempts to downplay the seriousness of the virus and hide the true extent of the disease will be fatal for some. POLITICO reports that "the government's incapacity to conduct widespread testing slowed diagnoses, creating chains of infection. It also deprived epidemiologists of a map that could have told them how far and how fast the virus was traveling and where they should concentrate efforts to slow it down."

This is just the latest evidence that Donald Trump will do anything to ensure he wins re-election and keeps a grip on power, whether it's deliberately enabling an epidemic in a wildly misguided effort to keep himself from getting blamed or abusing the powers of his office to bully our international allies into opening sham investigations into his political rivals. We cannot allow him to keep getting away with it. MAGA? What a joke.

Question: Does the STABLE GENIUS bear full responsibility for the medical/financial disaster, we Americans are now facing?

Answer: ABSOLUTELY.

The self-anointed "GENIUS" had numerous forewarnings of the impending disaster, yet because of his personal self-interests he did nothing except hesitate, and fire the medical experts/scientists who had been installed by President Obama, ready to act upon a crisis similar to what we are now facing.

Had this GENIUS been more concerned about the American people and their well being than he did for his electability, financial interests, hotels, casinos, golf courses, we wouldn't be in this mess.

The GENIUS bears fullest responsibility for the impending deaths of Americans. Be assured that the children of the GENIUS will be well protected with our taxpayer dollars, and looked after by the best medical team money can buy---unlike you, me and our families.

**A War Crime President** March 20

The latest BS con-job from our self anointed "genius" president: He's a wartime president!

His sick mind and fundamental ignorance of history apparently caught sight of the fact that Americans are hesitant to remove a real president while we are involved in a real shooting war.

Well, Donald, you self-anointed genius, we're not in a shooting war.

We're involved in a war of economic failure - due to your policies. And a war on disease in which your negligent failure to take preemptive steps to hamper the speed of the virus, is killing people.

You need to change your language from "I'm a wartime president" to "I'm a war crime president" much more fitting to your actions - which certainly demand a war crime trial - with fitting penalties.

**Trump Virus** April 8

He is a disaster. Big time. Frankly were his ignorance and arrogance only affecting his personal health, I wouldn't give a hoot. Sadly it's threatening death to millions of Americans. Don the Con had access to information about the pandemic in early January. He could have taken defensive action three months ago and ordered the needed testing and equipment, but he ignored the warnings and did nothing. Nero fiddled while Rome burned. Why must we suffer a Nero type disaster? Why, because Donald in his own words is a stable genius, smarter than all the scientists and doctors in the country? His recent public statement gives us the answer to Donald's brilliance.

*Statement by Donald Trump 3/9/2020 on the Coronavirus disaster*

"I like this stuff... I really get it. People are surprised that I understand it. Every one of these doctors said, 'How do you know so much about this?' Maybe I have a natural ability. Maybe I should have done that instead of running for president."

Oh dear God, what did we do to bring him on us? Take him away please! Out of sight! Out of hearing!

Please quickly find the vaccine for the *Trump Virus.*

**He loves dictators, like Putin, and we don't.** April 10

Face it fellow Americans. He's not one of us.

He has orange hair--we don't. He sexes porn queens while his wife is carrying "his(?) child" He shares beers with Brauhaus Nazis--we don't. He loves dictators, like Putin, and we don't.

Face it, he's not one of us, so what is he if he is not an American? His orange hair definitely types him as an orange haired orangutan that was banished from it's group. Shall we grant him US citizenship? A recent poll (taken of Americans not brain dead) showed 1% wanted to admit him to US citizenship. The 1% consisted of members of his own family and numerous felons presently in jail.

HEIL DON--be gone!

**Your Suicide by Voting For Trump** April 17

READER: If you're thinking of committing suicide (upon the current dismal world situation) by ingesting poisons the purchase of which will tap your bankroll--for example poisons such as Arsenic, Belladonna, Strychnine, Cyanide, Thallium. WELL, DON'T BOTHER! Our idiot in the White House, the one who self-proclaims himself a "STABLE GENIUS" is right on track for your suicide, my suicide, all of our suicides.

Unfortunately the "our" may well exclude his, Ivanka's, Melania's, Erik's, Don Jr's, Jared's demise. To be successful in protecting your bankroll while still seeing you readied for burial, a simple procedure. VOTE FOR THE "CONMAN" IN 2020. You will save a lot of costly suicide dollars.

The "con man" has already given you the path he would follow in 2020 and thereafter. Get your Will updated. He's moving along the path of mutual suicide. His most recent step being failure to alert the nation on the Coronavirus epidemic—DESPITE HIS CABINET MEMBERS HAVING GIVEN HIM WRITTEN ALERTS. OOPS, I ALMOST FORGOT "DON THE CON" DOESN'T READ, HE TRUSTS TO HIS MARVELOUS BRAIN. That could involve one of the greatest jokes of the century, if it doesn't kill us first.

# Dogs are being trained to sniff out coronavirus cases

Original concept by Richard Castellane

**KIMMEL and SHORT** May 14

Trump projects how sorry he is for the Corona epidemic. I personally don't believe him, but that's not the point of this letter. What concerns me is that he has exhibited gross negligence in handling the Corona matter--from the very first. He was given numerous warnings as to what could ensue but he did nothing. Preparation, forewarning went down the toilet bowl in the john adjoining the oval office. How you might ask should the American public treat Trump on this issue?

In my opinion the answer lies in the fate(s) of Admiral Kimmel and General Short, who were the military overseers at Pearl Harbor. The Japanese attack was devastating. Kimmel and Short had more than sufficient warning as to precautionary measures that should have been taken. Rather than take such measures they lined up their ships and planes in perfect order for them to be destroyed by Japanese aircraft.

The forewarning was akin to that received by our "STABLE GENIUS", Donald Trump prior to the Coronavirus epidemic. The end result for Kimmel and Short--they were removed from their commanding positions and never thereafter were trusted with commanding a military force in combat. Ask yourselves a simple question--should Trump after committing such gross negligence relative to the Coronavirus be allowed to command this great nation, the United States of America? My view, NEVER! He deserves that answer, election day is this coming November.

**MESSAGE TO OUR MILITARY** May 6

It's time for our MILITARY CHIEFS to let that "WOULD BE DICTATOR" sitting in the White House know that they will oppose with all forces at their command - any and all attempts by the CON MAN, aka DONALD TRUMP to overstay his time in the White House, WITH FULL FORCE, ON BEHALF OF OUR CONSTITUTION AND DEMOCRACY.

## OUR DRAFT DODGING COWARD May 18

The great Con-artist, widely known as Donald Trump, claims that his wearing of a mask (to fend off the Coronavirus) would send a message of WEAKNESS. I suggest Mr. Trump, if your self-proclaimed "stable genius" brain can deal with basic memory issues, to go back in time when you avoided the draft and thus avoided serving in Vietnam. Real bullets there, Don, not Champagne cocktails at Mar-a-Lago. You're now concerned about weakness? –don't want to project weakness by wearing a mask? What do you call it Don when you get your rich daddy to contact one of his tenants(renting a shop in daddy's development), to write a letter for review by your local draft board. The tenant, a shop chiropractor that one can't find any history on, let alone board certification. You finagled your draft status while thousands of Americans went, and fought (with many dying) in Vietnam. Your actions in avoiding combat are indicative of true WEAKNESS—by you---BIG TIME.

## MILITARY CHIEFS--ARMY, NAVY, AIR FORCE May 22

Take your heads out of the sand and wake up. It's beyond the time that you should have let that neo dictator (aka Donald Trump) know that you will oppose all attempts by him to overstay his time in the White House. Do any of you seriously think he will voluntarily pack up and leave after being defeated at the polls? He's given us warnings galore as to his dictatorial intentions. Better yet his former crony, Michael Cohen, has stated, "Given my experience working for Mr. Trump, I fear that if he loses in 2020, that there will never be a peaceful transition of power."

As Americans, we must heed the man who really got to know Trump. We fail to heed Michael Cohen at our own peril. I call upon you to inform Trump what he will face if he seeks to impede a peaceful transition of power. FORCE, AND YET MORE FORCE UNTIL TRUMP SCURRIES BACK TO HIS MAR-A-LAGO!!

## TRUMP LIES & AMERICANS DIE May 26

President Donald Trump has repeatedly blamed former President Barack Obama for his own administration's mishandling of the coronavirus pandemic. "The last administration left us nothing," Trump said.

But the St. Louis Post-Dispatch found that Trump's own budget documents show the opposite — exposing what it called "a lie of colossal Trumpian proportions." The newspaper's editorial board said the Trump administration told Congress that the Obama administration left it with everything needed for a pandemic — and sought big budget cuts from the programs as a result.

Trump's 2020 budget asked Congress to cut the pandemic preparedness budget by $102.9 million, part of $595.5 million in requested cuts to public health preparedness and response outlay.

"Obama left office with an unblemished record of building up the nation's pandemic preparedness," the newspaper said. "Trump systematically sought to dismantle it." Trump has since blamed his predecessor for lack of personal protective equipment and testing supplies, saying "our cupboards were bare. We had very little in our stockpile."

But the newspaper said a chart provided by the Trump administration with the budget shows that by 2016 — Obama's final year in office — the nation's public health emergency preparedness was at least 98% on every key measure. "That's by the Trump administration's own assessment," the Post-Dispatch said.

"If the cupboard was bare, it's because Trump swept it clean."

## OUR SELF ANOINTED STABLE GENIUS IS KILLING YOUR CHILDREN May 26

For mom's and dad's who receive the dreaded telegram---"We regret to inform you that your son/daughter has fallen in service of his/her duty to the United States of America."......

Such be the shattering comment denoting mourning, loss, heartbreaking memories. However there's an unstated implied section of the telegram that must be faced---THAT your son/daughter fell in action, never to return to you, because our glorious, draft dodging, stable genius president, followed his ongoing policy of alienating nations that once were our supporters--to the point that they have become hardened to our plight----to the detriment (death included) of your children. Under Trump our democracy has become but a vague memory. Nations that were once our supporters are no longer such.

When you go to the polls in November keep in mind that a Trump presidency can prove fatal to your child. Certainly, not fatal to the children of our self serving president. They'll have the fullest sanctuary under his corpulent body.

# MP TAX RETURN SHOWS HE SPENT $70,000 ON HIS HAIR STYLE.
## HE DEDUCTED IT AS AN EXPENSE!

Original concept by Richard Castellane

# Which hair style do you prefer? Send your vote to Republican National Comm
## 310 First Street SE, Washington, D.C

**GENERAL MATTIS SPEAKS OUT** June 5

THAT BUM IN THE WHITE HOUSE IS INTENT ON DESTROYING OUR DEMOCRACY. GENERAL MATTIS' STATEMENT WAS PROFOUND. WILL ALL WHO ARE READING WHAT I'VE WRITTEN HERE STOP ADDRESSING THAT RAT AS "MR PRESIDENT" THERE IS NO LAW OR RULE THAT MAKES A MR. PRESIDENT MANDATORY. SO PLEASE, FROM HERE ON, ADDRESS HIM AS "TRUMP" OR "MR. DON THE CON TRUMP". THE CHOICE IS OURS. HE SHOWS THE AMERICAN PEOPLE NOT AN IOTA OF RESPECT, I WILL GIVE TRUMP THE SAME RESPECT HE SHOWS MY FELLOW CITIZENS. WE ARE AMERICANS. OUR TRADITION IS ONE OF RESPECTING THOSE WHO ARE WORTHY OF IT. TRUMP IS UNWORTHY OF IT.

**Trump's Hatred Knows No Bounds** June 26

He is now dead set on taking from us Obamacare protections relative to preexisting conditions. YOU CAN BET YOUR BOTTOM DOLLAR SIMILAR ACTIONS ARE NOT OCCURRING, AND WILL NOT OCCUR, RELATIVE TO HIS, IVANKA'S, DON JR'S, ERIK'S, BARRON'S, MELANIA'S HEALTH CARE. Simply put, he doesn't give a tiddly squat for you, me, the American public. He's all for Trump and we as Americans should be deeply ashamed in having him as our president. Hopefully the forthcoming election will tell the world what we really think of him--that he is selfish, crude, the worst example of a leader that we've ever had. He certainly is not a president.

**A bounty on American Soldiers?** June 28

Trump is a traitorous bastard!

**Slip and Slide** June 29

An eel has nothing on him. He's a master of the "Slip and Slide Tango". But this time he's been caught. The American people seem to excuse a lot from trump, but acts of treachery and treason, putting young American lives in danger--no way! No forgiveness. The "Slip and Slide Tango" won't work this time Donald, won't distract us. So Americans face it, Trump is a traitor, a treasonous low life. As commander of our armed forces he comes under the Military Code of Justice 18US Code Sec 2381 and as follows:

"Whoever owing allegiance to the United States, levies war against them or adheres to their enemies, giving them aid and comfort within the United States or elsewhere, is guilty of treason and shall suffer death, or shall be imprisoned not less than five years and fined under this title but not less than $10,000, and shall be incapable of holding any office under the United States.

Trump is not exempt from the law. None of us is exempt from the law. Treat him accordingly.

**Slimicus Trumpitis** June 30

If Pence and Trump knew or should have known of the bounties being placed by the Russian government on the heads of young American soldiers fighting in Afghanistan, I must make a wish, one that I never thought I could make. I wish that the deaths of both Pence and Trump be ultra painful, and prolonged. Pence, that mysterious presence anchored in mediocrity had a duty. It was a duty that went beyond anything owed to "Don the Con". It was a duty to stand up and tell us, the American people, what was necessary to preserve the lives of young American soldiers. Pence has been submerged in Trumpian slime--far too long. He has caught the slime. It permeates his entire circulatory system. In some ways he's an even more dangerous fascistic figure than his master.

PS. A new word for Webster's--"Slimicus Trumpitis." A sickening disease which if not eliminated in its infancy, can cause life threatening infections.

# TRUMP DENIES ANY CONNECTION WITH THE RUSSIANS
## (LIKE INTERFERING WITH OUR ELECTIONS). REALLY DON?

Original concept by Richard Cas

Original concept by Richard Castellane

**Trump and the Testing Mess** July 1

Reports indicate that testing for the Coronavirus has broken down with endless lines, cars running out of gas while waiting, no food. A mess but you can bet your last dollar our self-proclaimed stable genius has provided rapid testing for his precious sons, daughter, friends. No lines for them. Were it the time of the French Revolution, they would all be standing before the guillotine. No waiting, just put your neck in the slot and WHOOPEE, your testing for the virus is over. Just wishful thinking...

**Military Speak Out** July 3

Some 10 months back I did an opinion letter setting forth an issue that is now at the forefront. The issue being what Trump's actions could be if he lost the forthcoming election. I ask that you read the letter that I wrote (see below). Also that you add the machinations available to Trump in the INSURRECTION ACT OF 1807 (see below). It appears clear that Trump will seek a continuation of an elicit, ill begot presidency--all to the diminution of AMERICAN DEMOCRACY.

I am writing this to retired high level military because the threat posed by Trump to our democracy, is all too real, too likely to happen. So what can you, retired military, do about it? I suggest you review your military oaths of allegiance to support the CONSTITUTION OF THE UNITED STATES--AGAINST ALL ENEMIES FOREIGN AND DOMESTIC.

The nation looks to you to set the example by speaking out NOW, NOT LATER WHEN IT MIGHT BE TOO LATE. Trump's playbook mirrors that of Adolf Hitler. Trump's methodology to keep control of the government, despite an election defeat is clear. The wouldbe dictator can be thwarted. Hitler could have been thwarted had what I am suggesting now had occurred during the so-called Munich conference and the British Prime Minister Nevil Chamberlain's proclamation that he had insured, after discussion with Hitler, "Peace in our time".

Wake up retired military. Speak up and stop our Hitlerian clone before it's too late. Time is running out. The impact of your words to the American public--is incalculable.

### On the Folly of Ignoring Constitutional Rights July 4

Sadly what I'm going to say will only be meaningful to maybe one out of every hundred Americans. But I must set this down because I believe it is related to the greatest single threat to American Democracy.

I have made a serious review of Trump's present horn blowing--on the state of the US economy-- (ie. employment numbers). Trump's blowhard presentation the other day of unemployment numbers, reminded me of the bombast practiced by Adolf Hitler some 90 years ago. Hitler touted German economic gains in the 1930s as the answer to German greatness. It was also touted as the direction Germans should follow under the leadership of "Herr Hitler". Unfortunately for the German people Hitler in his mesmerizing verbalization left out the most important thing--that while building the German economy under his Nazi regime, HItler was also setting in motion the imposition of all the major elements to destroy a democracy. Trump is following the Hitlerian road map--including destruction of the First Amendment, Free Press, Due Process, Respect for Diversity of Opinion, Humane Treatment of Minorities,....

Trump's bombast daily continues while he's slipping a Nazi inspired elixer into our stew. If only Americans could understand what Germans didn't--that while economic news may be palatable, if it exists during diminution of the rights of a free people, then it encompasses the coup de gras(a final killing blow) to American Democracy.

### A Good Night's Sleep July 6

If you want to return to a good night's sleep, a sleep free of bone chilling anxiety as to what "Don the Con" (AKA Trump) has now done or not done-- then for heaven's sake boot him out of the presidency so all of us can lessen the daily anxiety we experience because of the Con-man.

### Schools Must Reopen? July 13

Trump and DeVos demanded schools reopen by threatening to cut off billions of dollars in federal funding, much of which goes to low-income schools. Trump screamed, "SCHOOLS MUST REOPEN! Kid's can bear it-- their immune systems are "so powerful and so strong".

Trump wants things to be back to normal before the election. But they can't be. The pandemic is breaking out bigger and badder than ever.

If the Trump administration was genuinely concerned about single working women it would support them financially until this is over instead of sending them to jobs and their children to schools where they can catch a deadly virus. Does he want to kill your children?"

Barron Trump's school, St. Andrew's Episcopal School is working reopening but with a tiny number of children in each class. Public schools can't do this, their classrooms are overcrowded as it is and without any additional government support, Trump is ordering that you march your kids through the gates of hell, so that he can be re-elected and wreak havoc on us all over again. AS TO YOUR CHILDREN, HE DOESN'T GIVE A HOOT. They are canon fodder, providing cover while he sees to his business concerns, gambling casinos, golf courses, hotels and PRESIDENTIAL ASPIRATIONS!

**Don the Con is a Nazi** I July 29

AMERICANS WAKE UP--BEFORE IT'S TOO LATE. He is a remnant Nazi, who has defied the passage of time-- who your grandfathers fought on the beaches of Normandy, at the Remagen Bridge, in the Hurtgen Forest, during the Battle of the Bulge. DON IS A NAZI, MAKE NO MISTAKE ABOUT IT.

**To the Trump Mice Amongst Us** August 3

You call yourselves Americans? A part of the land of the free, home of the brave. What a joke. You're about as brave as a gutless mouse, and as far as you being part of the land of the free, well, Don the Con has daily rubbed your noses in his s---t and you let him do it--continually. Free? About as free as a German who criticized the Fuhrer in 1940.

What is most disturbing and indicative of gutlessness is your constantly addressing the con man as Mr President-- even after he ongoingly insults loyal Americans and our Constitution. The Con Man deserves not an iota of respect. Designating him as "Mr. President" is to show homage, respect for one who constantly, unashamedly stands for the worst of all--PURE UNADULTERATED TYRANNY, ALSO KNOWN AS NAZIISM.

I feel "DON THE CON" is a much better designation. Your view?

**Tyrants in History** August 14

Donald Trump is not the first tyrant. Freedom loving peoples have been required to deal with tyrants from the earliest arrival of human beings on this planet. BUT, Donald Trump is unique because the environment he's arrived at has noted itself as a monument for world admiration because of its adherence (up til now) to profound principles of democracy. The list of tyrants who have received the proverbial middle index finger are as follows:

- Muammar Gaddafi (killed by his own people)
- Saddam Hussein (executed after trial by his own people)
- Adolf Hitler (Subject of numerous assassination plots)
- Benito Mussolini (executed by his own people, hung from his heels in Milan)
- Idi Amin (ousted from power by the president of a neighboring country)
- Nicolae Ceausescu (executed by firing squad by his own people)
- Slobodan Milosevic (died during his trial before the World Court in the Hague)
- Jean-Claude Duvalier (died, heart attack, after return from 25 year exile)
- Ferdinand Marcos (died in exile)
- Hosni Mubarak (died after being deposed by popular unrest)
- A name yet to be added, (your choice) for his actions in destroying our Democracy.

**Crimes** August 18

Trump's interference with Americans' right to vote (ie. He's admitted motivation to interfere) is a criminal offense of a MOST SERIOUS NATURE. A massive number of states--through their Attorney General's offices must bring action against Trump. The statute dealing with the offense can call for, amongst other things, JAIL TIME (OF UP TO 12 MONTHS). Query, what is the Democratic leadership waiting for? Despite what Trump's hand picked judges might decide, there must be a public outcry, a scream of shattering proportions. There must be such if we are not to lose the last vestiges of a free society. Trump is a fascist dictator and we must get rid of him for the good of Democracy. The "UP TO 12 MONTHS IMPRISONMENT MUST BE FOLLOWED, SEEN TO ITS FULFILLMENT."

**A Wake up Call to Republican Politicians** August 18

If there is any desire on your part to continue in governmental service--heed the following: If, as seems very probable, your Donald is swept from office and by a landslide, your political status/clout goes bottom up. In other words you become dead meat.

If prior to the election you have taken positions supportive of "Don the Con's" fascistic, dictatorial, anti-US Constitution provisions, you will be noted as a "Trump-pet". You will reap the negative reward of having been supportive of a would-be dictator, a would-be king, a would-be NAZI. Such would be your political demise. But it need not be--if you now disassociate from "Don the Con"! Not only will you be doing the right thing for Democracy, but at the same time you'll be preserving your future.

**Crime Boss** August 18

Crime Boss 'Don the Con' Trump admitted on Thursday that he opposed additional funding for the United States Postal Service in order to make it more difficult to deliver mail-in ballots. Congressional negotiations over stimulus aid were held up in part because of Democratic proposals to provide $3.6BN to states to run elections and $25BN in aid to the postal service. Trump, who has falsely claimed that widespread mail-in voting will lead to fraud, suggested that without the funding it would be harder to vote by mail. Trump knows he is about to lose and will stop at nothing to steal the election. "They need that money in order to have the post office work so it can take all of these millions and millions of ballots," Trump said in an interview with Fox. "If they don't get it, that means you can't have universal mail-in voting because they're not equipped to have it." Trump and his donor-stooge "postmaster general" have slowed down the mail, removed mailboxes and ordered that 700 high speed sorting machines be removed immediately. In letters sent to all 50 states, lawyers for the USPS informed them that it may not be able to meet deadlines for delivering ballots. The USPS Code of Regulations states, "Whoever knowingly and willfully obstructs or retards the passage of the mail shall be fined or imprisoned not more than six months or both".

"Gangsters are presently occupying the White House but you ain't seen nothing yet. Just wait, God forbid, if Trump wins the 2020 election. He will turn this great Democracy into a gangster nation worthy of a Dutch Schultz, an Al Capone, a Bernie Madoff, and you can throw an Adolf Hitler into the stew."

Original concept by Richard Cast

**On Cindy McCain's on her late husband John McCain's friendship with Joe Biden.** August 21

That was so very significant to the upcoming election. It represented what a Democracy is supposed to be-- mutual respect and courtesy between ideological opponents. Donald Trump doesn't have a clue. To continue with Trump would represent the triumph of tyranny to the detriment of all Americans, present and future.

August 31 From the day Trump became president of the United States, all matters affecting our daily lives have become worse, day by day. Our need for some form of reasonable normalcy has been resoundingly smashed by a president whose "tweets", hour by hour, sew disunity, violence and most significantly the weakening of all major aspects of our Democracy.

We are becoming disunited, close to the point of no return. Daily tranquility, calmness, peacefulness, serenity are something we can only relate to as having occurred---in the past. It might be wise for the reader to ask him/ herself how frequently during the presidency of Trump, have you had a good night's sleep—no mental anguish, no tossing or turning, no waking up in a cold sweat. Donald Trump is not only a national disaster, but upon his pathetic example as a leader, he has become an international one.

From my university days at Princeton I have always been interested in the rise of Adolf Hitler, his attaining the position of Reisefuhrer, his demise, and where he took the German people with him—DOWNWARD—IN DESTRUCTION. I SEE AN ENORMOUS SIMILARITY BETWEEN ADOLPH HITLER AND DONALD TRUMP. BEING FAMILIAR WITH HITLER'S POSITIONS AS TAKEN IN HIS "MEIN KAMPF" I say without hesitation that Trump is following Hitler's playbook very very closely. The lying, the cheating, the stealing, the demeaning, the falsities of Hitler are part of the Trump tactic. Our own naïveté in closing our eyes to what Donald Trump really is, will end up causing our own demise.

GOD BLESS AMERICA---IF THERE STILL IS AN AMERICA AFTER THE ELECTION OF 2020.

**Traitor** September 8

    It's now becoming all too clear, Trump is an employee of the Russian Secret Service. All of his methods are right out of the Russian playbook. I scream, with the hope that some of you will pick up the truth, "DONALD TRUMP IS THE GREATEST TRAITOR THIS COUNTRY HAS EVER HAD. Let us now pin the Russian Order of the Red Star Medal on Trump's lapel. Oops sorry ...I slipped with the pin.

**To date, Trump has made more than 20,000 false or misleading claims.**

Here is the lie for today. Enjoy! "I've rebuilt the military, 2.5 trillion dollars." And, "I got them raises like no President before!" Trump frequently suggests this money is all for new equipment, but he's just adding together three years of budgets created by Nancy Pelosi passed in the normal course of business.

**Joe Biden, please make this statement:** "If you elect me as your president, I promised to take Putin down. In my 1st week, I will ask for a detailed briefing by our top security operations into the methods that the Russians have used to interfere with our election process. If I find anything negative, I will command our Cyber troops to immediately take down the entire Russian electrical, communication and banking grids. They will be permanently destroyed. Putin will feel the full force of the American Eagle's talons. The age of Trump's Russian Appeasement ends January 20th, 2021! Into the garbage can with Trump's appeasement of Putin."

Original concept by Richard Castellane

# The Law & Order Rat Fink

Original concept by Richard Castellane

**HE'S A PAPER TIGER? NO WAY. HE'S A PAPER MOUSE.** September 8

I'm deeply saddened by what this country, I love so dearly, is becoming. I once gloried in America. Proud beyond words. As a second generation American I was, first hand, living the American dream. Highest level education, graduate of Princeton University--my world steeped in ideas, discussion, art. As a second career (I liked challenges) I went to law school and eventually became a lawyer. In law school I was enthralled by Constitutional issues. I found great decisions by our Supreme Court on issues of due process, equal protection, and the First Amendment as breathtaking, beautiful in their fundamental decency. I was proud that such represented American ideals. But now under a Trump regime of ongoing tyranny I am very fearful of what we are becoming. I find it difficult to understand why so many in the Republican party (ie I am a registered Republican) sit on their hands while Trump, piece by piece, dismantles our great Democracy.

As a writer, I have been fascinated for years, with the story of the WHITE ROSE--a group of highly intelligent young Germans who actively opposed Hitler during the 1940s. They expressed through their writings that opposition. Always before these young people was the specter of death by guillotine, which was exactly what some of them experienced. I fail to understand what profound loss anyone today would face by publicly opposing Trump. He is a paper mouse, ready to be toppled from his paper throne. He fakes strength and through such appears to have bamboozled fellow Republicans into fear of him. SHAME ON YOU! If only you were of the ilk of the White Rose.

**CHURCHILL V. TRUMP** September 14

Donald Trump within the last several days "attempted" to compare himself to one of the greatest orators and statesman of our time--Winston Churchill. A simple comparison of their oratory places Trump's assertion in the garbage can. The following are two examples of Trump's and Churchill's leadership.

"We shall fight on the beaches, we shall fight on the landing grounds, we shall fight in the fields and in the streets, we shall fight in the hills; we shall never surrender..."

Commentary:

Can anyone believe that the mental zombie presently occupying the White House would dare to compare his actions to those of Winston Churchill? I'm firmly convinced, upon various criteria set forth in MAYO CLINIC writings, that (while they never name Trump directly) the criteria for SEVERE CHRONIC NARCISSISM FITS Trump TO A TEE. His bizarre behavior is following him about.---his actions are based on severe mental illness. You, me, our families are in great danger. Donald Trump is irrational, and HE HAS HIS FINGER ON THE NUCLEAR BUTTON. Think about that, for a little more time than the usual American attention span.

**RESEARCH REVEALS 13% OF AMERICANS ARE SUPERSTITIOUS** September 15

I don't think I'm superstitious--don't think so, BUT THERE ARE JUST TOO MANY AWFUL THINGS happening to America and Americans--since Trump became president.

Really bad things, like disasters, hurricanes, floods, forest fires, diseases--you name it. His presidency has been a disaster for the well being of Americans. Ever think THAT TRUMP MIGHT JUST BE THE CAUSE? Superstitious coincidence?

Maybe, but I'm not going to gamble. So, come election time, I'm going to vote to deny Trump getting another four years in the White House.

If I were to go with Trump there would just be too many ladders I'd have to walk under, too many.

**WAKE UP!** September 18

It's more than just simple politics. It's the actions of a President devoted to seeing the destruction of America.

YOUR vote in November shall either be for Democracy, or for the continued development of authoritarianism--better known as Naziism. Make no mistake about it, Trump's point of departure is to establish a form of Naziism in this wonderful country. To stand against Trump is to stand against ongoing chaos and dictatorship--IN THE NAZI MODE! Trump's responsibility for hundreds of thousands of deaths from the Coronavirus shall be but child's play to the millions who can die if he is reelected. Never forget, he has serious mental problems (well defined under criteria from the noted medical institution--the Mayo clinic), and with several hail marys, he has his finger on the nuclear button.

**COVID IS GOOD?** September 19

Trump said Covid-19 might be a "good thing" because it would stop him from having to shake hands with "disgusting people", according to a former top adviser to US vice president Mike Pence. Olivia Troye, who served on the White House coronavirus task force, is the latest ex-member of the Trump administration to urge US voters to stop him winning a second term.

**PATRIOT TRAITOR** September 25

**"Give me liberty or give me death"** decried American Patriot Patrick Henry in 1775 rallying the Virginia militia to join the fight against the British. Sounds corny today but it was the noble battle cry of a people striving to become free from tyranny. A peaceful transfer of power is the key to our Democracy. Without a peaceful transfer, we become at the very instant, a full blown dictatorship, a clone of Hitler's Nazi State. I speak only for myself but if such an instance occurs following our forthcoming election, I will do what was once for me unthinkable - and take up arms and proudly repeat the cry of Patrick Henry.

My 87 year old legs are not very reliable but I will do my best to topple the tyrant Trump.

**Conman** September 28

Did I hear you right? You're saying you won't leave unless your conditions are met, again spitting on our Constitution? Well mister, think this over: When you lose, you are going to leave. You can bet on it. Even if I have to kick my boot up your fat ass. I take your evil very personally. I believe millions of Americans do likewise. Good legs on good boots vs. your fat ass. Don't tempt us! You don't show the slightest respect for the people. You're not the president, you're a con. And now with the release of your tax returns, it's clear that the only reason you want to be re-elected is so that you aren't indicted. Jail waits for your fat ass.

**Trump owes Putin** September 29

Corruption. It's staring at us, clearly so. Intelligence Chief Dan Coates thought so; Putin watchers thought so too. But now comes the proof: Our genius president (who would sell his soul for a bosomy blonde - or taking five strokes off his golf score) has sold us down the river. He never revealed his enormous debt which made him highly corruptible, unlike any president in history. Why didn't he reveal his vast debt before the last election? He knew Americans would have rejected him as being both a failed businessman and a stooge beholden to those to whom he personally owes $400,000,000 of debt. This emerging fact must reward this con man with the best of all consequences: The American people who steadfastly have backed him - can now see him clearly for the lying cheat that he has always been.

**Moral Depravity** September 30

Not satisfied playing with the lives of adults, Trump is now targeting the lives of our children. Recent revelations show where the Regime followed Trump's lies and commanded the CDC to downplay the risks of returning to school. Children are highly vulnerable to Covid and they are proven virus spreaders.

Trump's motive? As always, to gain political points - but this time, he's murdering the children. He doesn't care, he's happy to lead the lambs to slaughter without the slightest concern, if it enables him to remain in power.

Who amongst you trumpets has even the slightest conscious to prevent such an evil man from returning to the White House?

**Narcissism** October 9

Donald Trump is mentally ill. Several years back I wrote about his severe narcissism and what would eventually come from it. The mental illness that our nation is experiencing in Trump is what I predicted years ago. The most horrific part of my prediction was that, in his mental state he has his finger on the nuclear button. The odds now, for you and your family roasting in a nuclear cloud are much greater now than before Trump took office. For the survival of all Americans, VOTE HIM OUT!! SURVIVAL REQUIRES IT.

**Totalitarian State?** October 16

The basic issue in the upcoming election is not any of the particularized matters constantly before you. The basic issue is far more significant. It is the question, do we want to see a nation, our beloved nation, embrace principles inherent in a Democracy, OR do we want the installation of a government with an authoritarian (dictatorial) Trump as president--embracing principles of a Nazi, Totalitarian state.

**Gazprombank** October 22

The New York Times's blockbuster report on Trump's tax records has drawn attention to the fact that he is $421MM in debt coming due in the next 3-4 years. Who does he owe the money to? What favors does he owe?

According to White House sources, Trump flew into a rage and has been acting deranged, consumed by fear of the on-going investigation by the FBI, when it was revealed today by the German newspaper Der Spiegel, that Trump in fact owes the money to Vladamir Putin.

Details revealed that a Putin controlled bank, Gazprombank deposited half a billion dollars into the American subsidiary of Deutsche Bank at the same time that the bank made Trump loans, according to exclusively obtained confidential bank records.

The cash laundering relationship between the banks allowed the Russian government rubles to be converted to U.S. dollars and then deposited in Trump's account.

Trump must repay the loans in US dollars, which Putin will receive no doubt, in one of his many offshore accounts. Putin is considered the world's richest individual with nearly a trillion dollars in assets worldwide.

# UMP'S GRAVE DIGGERS OF DEMOCRACY

al concept by Richard Castellane

**Gravediggers** October 25

**I'm sick and tired of sensitivity.** It seems like the Democratic party is going into a fully apologetic stance relative to the matter of putting forth extra Supreme Court nominees if the Republicans pursue their path of voting on their nominee Amy Coney Barrett before the election. Let's say it as it is--**the American people** were cheated/fooled/lied to by Lindsey Graham who spoke **on behalf of the Republican party.**

It was a bald faced lie supported by Republican Congressmen upon their refusal to rebut it.

I for one don't like being lied to and I fully support the Democrats proposing extra Supreme Court nominees in answer to the Lindsey Graham/Republican party's/Donald Trump's **LIES!** A strong fist should be the answer to what the Republicans did--not apologetically beating around the bush. Graham on behalf of the Republican party (ie no protests to be heard from them) assured us, **THE AMERICAN PEOPLE,** that there would be no submission of Barrett's nomination before the forthcoming election.

**THEY LIED! Bigger than big time, they lied.** They put another nail in the coffin of American reliance on a politician's word.

**DAMN THEM! THEY ARE ALL GRAVEDIGGERS OF OUR GREAT DEMOCRACY! Vote them out! Have them flee into the swamp (i.e. hopefully malaria-infested) that they themselves have created, by their lies.**

## A POTENTIAL MOMENT OF TRUTH

October 27

*The following is a fictitious statement from Amy Coney Bryant.*

But what if it wasn't?

"To All Americans! By the time you read this, I will have been sworn in as a Justice of the US Supreme Court.

To be a Justice has been from my 1st day as a law student, my most recurring dream. There is now unfortunately a problem that sullies that dream.

Because of politics, my nomination and ascension to the nation's highest court has been rushed through just days prior to the upcoming election, a very contentious election. The reasons for the rush - all political - are that President Trump is betting upon my judicial history that I will decide several major cases, as the deciding vote, to his liking including his own election if it is contested; the end of the Affordable Care Act and a women's right to choice.

I am personally appalled that our Supreme Court which has always strived to remain above political influence has been torn apart and achieved a new low in respect by the American people. If I am good enough to be endorsed as a Justice <u>now</u> then I should be good enough to be endorsed after the election.

President Trump and Senate Majority Leader Mitch McConnell deserve my- and the American peoples' fullest contempt for destroying the faith that Americans still had in a non-political Supreme Court.

That faith has now become contempt. I hereby withdraw from the appointment of Associate Justice of the Supreme Court, asking that my name be resubmitted for consideration <u>after</u> the forth-coming election".

Justice Amy Coney Bryant

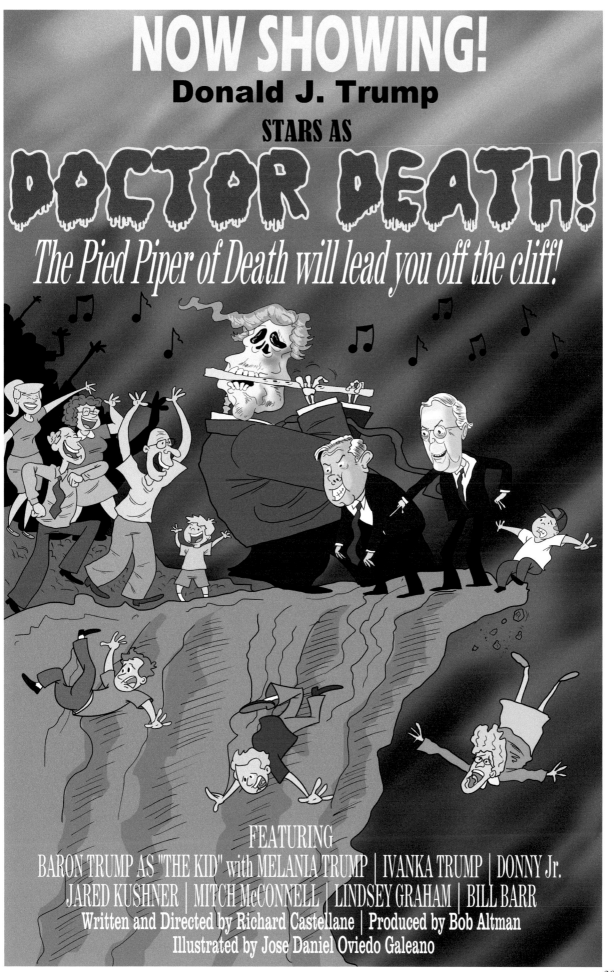

By Election Day November 3, 2020
Trump had made more than 25,000 false or misleading claims.

# Be Gone Don,
# Be Gone!

# The snake is out to kill us.
## He's already devoured American honor, integrity, truthfulness but there is an answer.

# In the Hope of Reconciliation Between the
# Two Parties and its Constituents

The election is over except for the expected screaming and tail-biting of Trump. But it's over. My hatred of Trump is set forth in the clearest terms within the "I Hate Trump" book.

However my hatred takes second place to the love I feel for American Democracy. Upon such, I implore our new President to be conciliatory whenever possible to the Republican Party. The fate and future of this country depends on such.

The principle to follow is to show a basic affection for all Americans, upon their being Americans, regardless of the positions they've taken in the past. Our commonality must be at the forefront. Only by such reconciliation can this country survive. I have several ideas in mind that I'll set forth in future letters.

The first however I can set forth now. Our new president should announce in one of his first speeches to the nation that he will be holding bi-weekly breakfast meetings with major Republican opposition members in order to discuss matters of disagreement, and agreement, with civility and with the objective of coming together--without bloodshed.

The theme must be we are **ALL** Americans.

**Richard Castellane**
Munnsville, NY

# A Fart in The Wind

Original concept by Richard Castellane

H LIKE THE SICKENING ODOR OF A FART IN THE WIND, IS THE STENCH OF "DON THE CON".
IT WILL LINGER--FOR A SHORT TIME LINGER, BUT THEN TO THE RELIEF
OF OUR NASAL PASSAGES FADE AWAY, NEVER TO BE SNIFFED AGAIN.

## Richard Castellane
Writer/Author/Executive Producer

A graduate of Princeton University, Department of Art and Archaeology, Castellane worked directly under world famous archaeologist Dr. Prof. Eric Sjoquist.

Thereafter, he performed graduate work at Columbia University under Professors Meyer Schapiro and Julius Held. Then Assistant to Hans Schaefer (noted old master's art dealer) where emphasis was on such old Masters as Rubens, Tiepolo, Rembrandt, Hals, etc. Opened gallery in New York City, Castellane Gallery and became notable for having amongst the earliest exhibitions of Pop Art (William Kent indicated in Lucy Lippards book "Pop Art" as Pre 1960), Sensory Art (artist Jo Roman where objects could only be felt not seen), Op Art (artists such as Ben Cunningham etc.), Installation and Psychedelic Art (Yayoi Kusama), and one of the earliest exhibitions of Earth artist Robert Smithson.

After his work in the art world, Castellane attended law school and became an Attorney. His greatest interest though was writing creative stories and screenplays, one of his first being "Little Hippino", the popular children's book.

Another of Castellane's screenplays, the football comedy "Hail Mary!", about a losing professional football team that buys up a school of sumo wrestlers to be made into offensive linemen, won the Audience Award at the Queens World Film Festival. The film is currently in distribution on Amazon and other digital platforms.

Other recent screenplays include "Corned beef and Cabbage", concerning a love affair between a corned beef and a cabbage that ends in the new St. Patrick's Day feast becoming salami and Brussels sprouts; and "Deedle the Dung Beetle", concerning a dung beetle colony that faces starvation when the "goodies" they usually gather become extinct.

Castellane's film "Irrefutable Proof" was awarded the "Golden Palm Award" for Best Picture as well as Best Cinematography and Best Actress at The Beverly Hills Film Festival and has been internationally released in 2018.

Printed in the United States
By Bookmasters